ABOUT PROJECT KNITWELL

PROJECT KNITWELL IS A NONPROFIT ORGANIZATION THAT AIMS TO BRING THE JOY OF KNITTING TO PEOPLE FACING DIFFICULT SITUATIONS. It was started by a mother as a result of her experience caring for her hospitalized infant daughter. She spent countless hours in the hospital, and found it very difficult to concentrate. After receiving a hand-knit sweater as a gift for her daughter, she renewed her own interest in knitting and believes that it provided a welcome distraction for her from the immediate worries related to her daughter's hospital stay.

Currently, Project Knitwell provides knitting instruction and materials to patients, family members and health care providers in several hospitals throughout the metro Washington DC area, in after-school programs for at-risk youth, and to cancer support groups in the community. Many of Project Knitwell's participants are caregivers.

In addition, Project Knitwell has participated in research about the therapeutic benefits of knitting for oncology nurses, and has developed a Resource Guide for the Young Knitter as well as a Guidebook to help others start a similar program. The organization's leadership and volunteer knitting instructors are a resource for helping others establish knitting programs in community sites. They also provide tips for teaching knitting to people in stressful situations, and information about the benefits knitting can provide.

For more information, visit us at www.projectknitwell.org, and like us on our Facebook page to keep up with news about Project Knitwell.

Mission Statement

Project Knitwell is a non-profit organization dedicated to bringing the joy of knitting and its therapeutic benefits to people facing stressful situations. Project Knitwell volunteers provide knitting instruction and quality materials in an effort to foster wellness, comfort, and community among patients, family members, medical staff, and others facing difficult circumstances.

INTRODUCTION

Why a booklet for Caregivers?

There are many guidebooks for learning to knit but this one is unique in two ways. First, it focuses on a specific population, the caregiver, and secondly it covers both knitting instruction and the reasons knitting has therapeutic benefits.

Caregivers are persons who take care of others, usually during a health crisis or other stressful situation. Some persons are employed as caregivers, while others, such as family members, neighbors, or friends are often thrust into the role. Project Knitwell knows from its experience in teaching knitting in health-care settings and from participating in a research study on Compassion Fatigue among Oncology Nurses, that caregivers are faced with a challenging role that often causes physical and mental stresses, such as anxiety, sadness, and fatigue. Self-care is necessary for the well-being of persons in caretaking roles. Knitting has been shown to help improve well-being.

This one-of-a-kind knitting guide will help caregivers learn to knit and to complete simple items that they will be proud to give or wear. Every effort has been made to create illustrations and explanations that are crystal clear, and the print and on-line resources have been selected with the caregiver in mind. First-person accounts from caregivers about knitting are provided as well as resources related to the many therapeutic benefits of knitting.

Carol Caparosa

Carol Caparosa
Founder, Project Knitwell

CONTENTS

ALL YARNS FEATURED IN THIS BOOK ARE LION BRAND® YARNS & MADE IN THE USA

KNIT AWAY YOUR STRESS

"Like meditation or prayer, knitting allows for the passive release of stray thoughts. The rhythmic and repetitive quality of the stitching, along with the sound of the needles clicking resembles a mantra." -Dr. Herbert Benson

THE COMFORT OF KNITTING

THE VERY PROCESS OF KNITTING BRINGS COMFORT. The rhythmic motion of the needles clicking and the feel of the yarn in one's hands can provide solace during the most trying times. Watching the stitches form, seeing a project progress, simply knowing you have something in your knitting bag that you can pull out and work on, are just a few of the reasons knitting can be a lifeline when the going gets tough. But is it actually beneficial to you? The answer is a definitive "Yes"!

NEWS FLASH: KNITTING IS GOOD FOR YOUR HEALTH. The media is all over it. Prestigious news outlets including *The Washington Post, The Wall Street Journal,* CNN, CNBC, and *Psychology Today* have all recently run features extolling the health benefits of knitting. (See Resources on page 45 for a list.)

Just what is it about the craft of knitting that is so beneficial to one's mental and physical wellbeing? Is it the repetitive motion? Is it the satisfaction of making something? Is it knitting's ability to take our attention away from our problems? It's all of the above and more!

In addition to anecdotal evidence supplied by just about any knitter you talk to, the benefits of knitting have been the subject of numerous research studies. (For testimonials from Project Knitwell knitters and others, see Ask a Knitter, page 13.)

KNITTING IS PREVENTATIVE MEDICINE. When it comes to handcrafts, Dr. Alton Barron, orthopedic surgeon and co-author of *The Creativity Cure: How to Create Happiness with Your Own Two Hands,* subscribes to the "use it or lose it" school of thought. "Sixty percent of the surface of the brain is committed to using the hands." Barron and his wife and co-author, Dr. Carrie Barron, a psychiatrist, have been studying the health benefits of creative pursuits for almost three decades. He contends that bimanual activities like knitting can create new neural pathways. "By using both hands simultaneously with fine dexterity, you are stimulating both hemispheres of the brain."

KNITTING CAN DECREASE STRESS LEVELS. In the early 1970s, Harvard Medical School professor and cardiologist, Dr. Herbert Benson, conducted a study on the positive health effects of meditation in which he observed that, like meditation, crafts that require concentration and repetitive motion such as knitting, can lower heart rate, blood pressure and overall stress levels. His findings were documented in his best-selling book, *The Relaxation Response*, which was pivotal in making mindfulness mainstream and is still considered a go-to resource on the subject. (More on mindfulness later...)

KNITTING CAN HAVE AN ANTI-DEPRESSANT EFFECT. More recently, British physiotherapist Betsan Corkhill undertook an extensive research project* that found knitting can improve personal and social wellbeing. Her 2013 study of knitters showed significant psychological and social benefits of the craft, which can contribute noticeably to quality of life. After knitting, 81.5 percent of respondents rated themselves as feeling "a little" to "very happy," and 67 percent of respondents rated the process or activity of knitting important in inducing feelings of calm and relaxation.

KNITTING CAN HELP ALLEVIATE EATING DISORDERS. A 2009 University of British Columbia study of women hospitalized with anorexia found that 74 percent said knitting lessened their fears and kept them from ruminating about their eating disorders. 74 percent lauded the calming aspects of the craft, while 53 percent said it provided satisfaction and a sense of accomplishment.**

KNITTING CAN DELAY MEMORY LOSS. In his 2012 study, Mayo Clinic professor and neuroscientist Yonas Geda discovered that seniors who engaged in knitting and other activities requiring concentration were 30 to 50 percent less likely to have mild cognitive impairment than those who did not. ***

AND KNITTING MAY SLOW THE ONSET OF ALZHEIMER'S DISEASE. The same study found that those who spent their 50s and early 60s reading, playing games and engaging in various craft hobbies, including knitting and quilting, had a 40 percent lower risk of memory impairment than those who didn't have hobbies.

According to the Alzheimer's Association, a staggering 1-in-9 Americans over the age of 65 has Alzheimer's disease, and as baby boomers age, that statistic will only increase. Geda believes that "aging does not need to be a passive process" and his studies conclude that leisure activities like knitting could delay dementia and fight PTSD. As if we needed more convincing that knitting is good for our health!

***See page 45 for reference sources.

THE YARN THAT BINDS

The relationship between knitting and Alzheimer's spans quite a scale between caregivers and those with the disease. On one end the caregivers can use knitting to help themselves psychologically and emotionally, having something that helps calm them and move them forward. On the other end knitting can become a way to connect with the person who has Alzheimer's, a very tactile shared experience with yarn and loving hands.

-David Babcock, the knitting runner and fundraiser for Alzheimer's Association

Knit Lit

THERE ARE MANY BOOKS THAT DELVE INTO THE GOODNESS OF KNITTING. HERE ARE SOME OF OUR FAVORITES:

Knit For Health & Wellness: How To Knit a Flexible Mind & More...
Betsan Corkhill
(Flatbear Publishing, 2014)

Love in Every Stitch: Stories of Knitting and Healing
Lee Gant
(Viva Editions, 2015)

The Relaxation Response
Dr. Herbert Benson
(William Morrow, 1975)

Knit Red: Stitching for Women's Heart Health
Laura Zander
(Sixth&Spring Books, 2012)

Knitting Yarns: Writers on Knitting
Ann Hood
(Norton, 2014)

Knitting Heaven and Earth: Healing the Heart with Craft
Susan Gordon Lydon
(Potter Craft, 2008)

The Knitting Way: A Guide to Spiritual Self Discovery
Linda T. Skolnik and Janice MacDaniels
(SkyLight Paths, 2005)

Mindful Knitting: Inviting Contemplative Practice to the Craft
Tara Jon Manning
(Tuttle, 2004)

Zen And The Art Of Knitting: Exploring the Links Between Knitting, Spirituality, and Creativity
Bernadette Murphy
(Adams Media, 2002)

Crochet Saved My Life: The Mental and Physical Health Benefits of Crochet
Kathryn Vercillo
(Self-published, 2012)

The Creativity Cure: How to Build Happiness with Your Own Two Hands
Carrie Barron, MD and Alton Barron, MD
(Scribner, 2012)

IF YOU FIND IT IN YOUR HEART
TO CARE FOR SOMEONE ELSE,
YOU WILL HAVE SUCCEEDED -Maya Angelou

KNITTING AND CAREGIVERS

THE MERRIAM-WEBSTER DICTIONARY DESCRIBES A CAREGIVER AS "A PERSON WHO PROVIDES DIRECT CARE (as for children, elderly people, or the chronically ill)". Being responsible for the daily care of a family member or friend can be a depleting and isolating experience. And while the job of professional caregiver can be rewarding, it is also a draining and high-stress career, filled with frequent sadness and loss.

DEPRESSION IS COMMON AMONG CAREGIVERS, both lay people and professionals, and burnout is a very real phenomenon. In general, people who are compassionate by nature are attracted to the so-called caring professions and often find it difficult to detach from their surroundings and influences. A condition called Compassion Fatigue, was first recognized in nurses in the 1950s. It is a disorder characterized by a gradual lessening of compassion over time and is common among individuals who work directly with trauma victims, such as nurses, psychologists and first responders. Sufferers can exhibit symptoms including hopelessness and negativity, a decrease in experiences of pleasure, constant stress, anxiety and sleeplessness. The underlying sense of hopelessness is especially common in, but not limited to, the field of oncology who are continually exposed to death and dying, grieving families, traumatic stories, severe physical pain, and strong emotional states, such as anger and depression in patients and family members. A study conducted at Medstar Georgetown University Hospital supports the literature that describes compassion fatigue as a real phenomenon among oncology nurses and demonstrates that knitting is a beneficial way to combat compassion fatigue.****

****See page 45 for reference sources.

Under any circumstances, chronic stress breaks down a person's immune system. According to the Alzheimer's Association, seventy-four percent of caregivers of people with Alzheimer's disease and other dementias reported that they were "somewhat concerned" to "very concerned" about maintain-ingtheir own health since becoming a

Get involved!

WANT TO START A KNITTING PROGRAM IN A HOSPITAL?

A learn-to-knit program can be hugely beneficial to patients, families, friends, clergy and professional caregivers alike. To learn how to start a group in your hospital, email info@knitwell.org to receive an electronic copy of their "How-To Guide on Establishing a Pediatric Knitting Program in a Hospital Setting."

caregiver. You don't want to get sick when you're a caregiver for someone else, so it's key that you take adequate care of yourself during this tough time.

HOW CAN KNITTING HELP?

It's natural to be worried about the patient's day-to-day condition, whether they are declining or improving. The rest of life's responsibilities don't stop, so things can feel out of control. It might seem counterintuitive to take up a new craft at a time when you are extra-stressed, but consider these factors:

• Knitting can be the ultimate self-care tool. It is something you can do just for yourself, by yourself, so it's a way to detach from the situation at hand.

• At the same time knitting can be a social activity to help alleviate the sense of isolation often associated with caring for someone who is ill. The act of knitting always attracts onlookers!

• **KNITTING IS PORTABLE.** Whether you're a patient, family member, friend or professional caregiver, you can pick up your knitting during breaks or between appointments, and you can do it virtually anywhere.

• **KNITTING BOOSTS SELF-ESTEEM.** Being unable to heal the people you love and/or are caring for can erode self-esteem so it's important to restore it in other ways. Once you've learned the basics, seeing a project progress is immensely satisfying, and the end product is praised and enjoyed by others.

• **KNITTING IS CREATIVE,** and creativity is necessary for wellbeing and balance.

The Power of Color

WHEN YOU ARE CHOOSING COLORS FOR YOUR PROJECT, THINK ABOUT WHO THE RECIPIENT OF THE FINISHED PIECE WILL BE AND CONSIDER THE COLOR'S SYMBOLIC MEANING

RED	PINK	BROWN	ORANGE	GOLD
Energy, strength, love, courage. Heart health.	Joy, friendship, femininity. Breast cancer awareness.	Stability, masculinity.	Happiness, success, endurance.	Illumination, wisdom.
YELLOW	**GREEN**	**BLUE**	**PURPLE**	**WHITE**
Cheerfulness, energy, confidence.	Healing, harmony, protection, hope, peace.	Stability, trust, loyalty, faith, tranquility.	Wisdom, dignity. Alzheimer's awareness.	Goodness, innocence, faith, safety, light.

MIND YOUR KNITTING

It seems like everyone is touting "mindfulness" these days. What exactly is it, and how can you be in it when you're in the midst of a family health crisis? And what does knitting have to do with it?

Mindfulness is often referred to as "being present" or being in the moment. In their book, *The Creativity Cure*, doctors Carrie and Alton Barron, call it "Mind Rest" - a time to relax your brain, ponder, putter and be still. Psychologist Mihaly Csikszentmihaly, describes it as flow: a few moments in time when you are so completely absorbed by an activity that nothing else seems to matter. Flow, he claims, is the secret to happiness.
For many people, knitting can be that happy place. A time when worries slip away, when the mind can focus on the rhythm of the needles, and the beauty of the fabric forming in your hands.

CARING FOR THE CAREGIVER

"Many caregivers share that they often feel alone, isolated, and unappreciated. Mindfulness can offer renewed hope for finding support and value for your role as a caregiver...It is an approach that everyone can use. It can help slow you down some so you can make the best possible decisions for your care recipient. It also helps bring more balance and ease while navigating the caregiving journey."

-Nancy L. Kriseman, *The Mindful Caregiver*: Finding Ease in the Caregiving Journey

According to Carrie Barron, MD and her husband Alton Barron, MD, authors of *The Creativity Cure – How to Build Happiness with Your Own Two Hands*, activities like knitting can create a "Mind Shift" even during times of extreme stress. Mind Shift is just what it sounds like, a way to shift your state of mind by introducing positive thoughts.

• **THE REPETITIVE MOTION OF KNITTING IS CALMING.** It can help alleviate some of the anxiety surrounding illness. Repetitive movements can slow down thought processes, enabling one to think more clearly, and even improve your mood and help manage worry associated with stress. (See "Mind Your Knitting", page 11.)

• **KNITTING GIVES A SENSE OF CONTROL** over something and can provide structure and purpose during a chaotic and uncertain time. You can't control illness but you can make decisions about your project.

• **BOTH LEARNING A NEW SKILL AND SEEING THE FINISHED KNITTED PRODUCT** give a feeling of satisfaction and achievement, which can help offset the frustrations of caring for someone who often isn't able to give back. And knitting is a lifelong skill, so once you've got the hang of it, you're hooked for life.

As knitting guru and philosopher Elizabeth Zimmerman observed in her classic book, *Knitting Without Tears* (Fireside Books, 1971), "Properly practiced, knitting soothes the troubled spirit, and it doesn't hurt the untroubled spirit either."

Ask a Knitter

PROJECT KNITWELL KNITTERS TALK ABOUT HOW KNITTING HELPED THEM

WHEN GIVEN THE CHOICE OF A MOVEMENT CLASS OR TO KNIT, I WILL KNIT. IT IS IMPORTANT TO ME. IT IS VERY SOOTHING.

-Mom of a 12-year old oncology patient

I often bring my knitting to work and stitch during quiet times during the shift. It also soothes me and helps me to be a better caregiver. -Laura, nurse in a dementia care unit

I knit at night when I wake up and am worried, and I feel better after a while.

-Tracy, mother of a pediatric patient

I look forward to knitting to relax and breathe... it really takes my mind off things. It gives me peace of mind. -Sabrina, mother of NICU patient

THIS REALLY MAKES ME CONCENTRATE AND TAKES MY MIND OFF OTHER THINGS.

-17-year old female patient

Knitting helped me get through my daughter's time in the NICU by giving me a support network with other moms in the preemie knitting group. Even though I could not even hold her for the first month, I poured my love into a sweater that fit her perfectly when she was ready to come home. -Abbi, mom of infant who was in NICU for 6 months

GETTING STARTED

WHEN YOU GET DOWN TO ABSOLUTE BASICS, KNITTING IS ALL ABOUT STICKS AND STRING, and you can certainly get started with just a ball of yarn and a pair of knitting needles. But like most things in life, it can get a whole lot more complicated. For this booklet, we've boiled it down to basics so that you can begin to experience the comfort of knitting right away!

WHAT YOU'LL NEED:

IT ALL BEGINS WITH YARN AND NEEDLES, BUT KNITTING COMES WITH A RANGE OF FUN TOOLS, LIKE THE ONES SHOWN BELOW. (YOU'LL ALSO NEED A CUTE PROJECT BAG IN WHICH TO CARRY YOUR KNITTING TO APPOINTMENTS AND VISITS!)

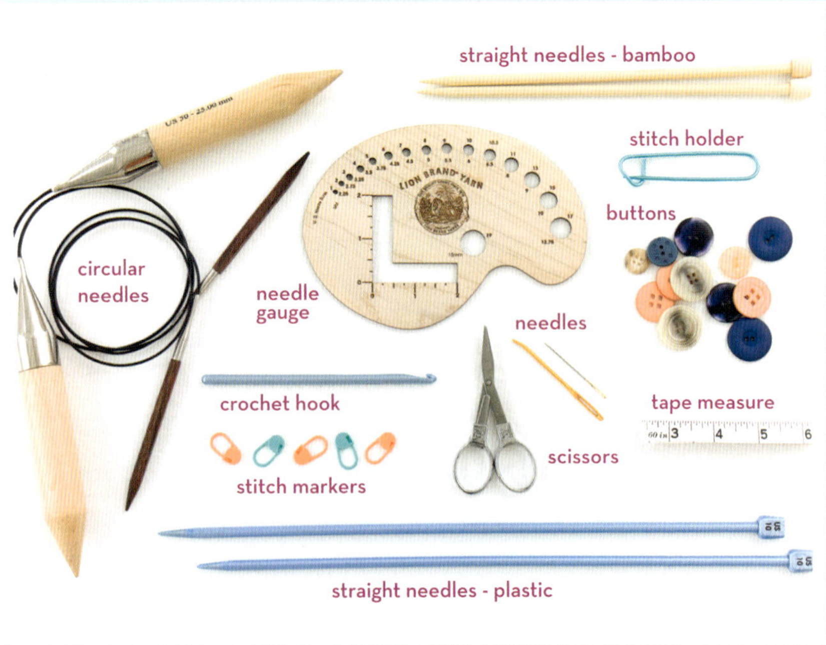

What's in a label?

The Craft Yarn Council of America has developed universal symbols that make reading a yarn label easy. You can pick up almost any skein or ball of yarn and be able to easily tell what the name and color of that yarn are, what weight it is, what the fiber content is, what the recommended needle size is, and even how to care for it once your project is complete.

YARN WEIGHT

Yarn comes in many weights, from the very finest lace-weights to bold mega-bulky yarns. Since it's easiest to learn on something in between, we've chosen two popular bulky yarns for all of the tutorials and patterns in this booklet.

NEEDLE SIZE

Another universal symbol that is on virtually every yarn label is the recommended needle and crochet hook size. (See "What the Heck is Gauge" page 16, for more on this subject.)

FIBER CONTENT

Allergic to wool? Looking for cotton? Crazy for cashmere? All fiber content is clearly indicated on the yarn ball label.

CARE AND LAUNDERING

Also on the label are those cute little symbols like the ones on purchased garments. Is the yarn machine washable? Can you put it in the dryer? There are many, many machine-washable yarns on the market, including the ones used in this booklet, but as you get into more expensive yarns including fancy novelty yarns and luxury fibers like alpaca, hand washing and even dry cleaning are often recommended.

WHAT THE HECK IS GAUGE?

The projects in this booklet are not that gauge-dependent, but once you are hooked on knitting, which you certainly will be, you'll need to pay attention to gauge because it affects the finished size of your knitted piece. If you don't get the pattern gauge, a garment, for example, will not come out to the intended size.

Gauge refers to the number of stitches and rows a knitter makes per inch using a certain yarn and needles. Gauge varies from person to person, so it is very important to make sure you are achieving the gauge your pattern recommends. If you are knitting with a thick yarn you'll make bigger stitches and have very few stitches and rows per inch. If you are knitting with a finer yarn, you'll make smaller stitches and have more stitches and rows per inch.

To make an accurate gauge swatch, cast on enough stitches to equal approximately four inches and work in pattern for four inches. Take your stitches off the needle and, without stretching the fabric, place a tape measure on your work and gently pin where the tape measure reads one inch. Count your stitches. Don't cheat. Make sure to count even a half or quarter of a stitch and include that into your gauge. If you have more stitches per inch than the gauge suggests, that means you are working too tightly; try a larger needle. If you have fewer stitches than the suggested gauge, your stitches are too loose; try a smaller needle.

Knit Speak!

COMMONLY-USED ABBREVIATIONS IN KNITTING

beg = beginning
dec = decreas(e)(s)(ing)
inc = increas(e)(s)(ing)
k = knit
k2tog = knit 2 stitches together
p = purl
rep = repeat
RS = right side
sl = slip
st(s) = stitch(es)
St st = Stockinette stitch
tog = together
WS = wrong side

KNIT, PURL… KNIT, PURL… KNIT, PURL…
IT'S LIKE A HEARTBEAT –Anna, oncology patient at a DC-area hospital

HOW-TO BASICS

WHAT YOU'LL NEED: TWO NEEDLES AND A BALL OF YARN. The basic techniques you'll need for the projects in this book are casting on, the knit stitch, the purl stitch and binding off. For more Learn-to-Knit tips, more advanced techniques, tutorials and videos, visit the **Learning Center** at **www.lionbrand.com**.

START WITH A SLIP KNOT

The slip knot serves as your first stitch when starting any knitting project. There are many ways to make a simple slip knit. Here is our favorite:

Make a loop with the yarn strand. Lay the loop in your right hand. Have the yarn coming from the ball to your left and the cut end of the yarn to your right.

Hold both yarn strands with your left hand, wrapping the yarn from the ball over your left index finger. Insert your right index finger and thumb into the yarn loop.

Reach through the loop and pull the yarn through, using your left index finger for tension. It may feel awkward at first, but once you get it, it's magic!

Gently pull to tighten the knot.

Place the loop from the slip knot onto one knitting needle. This is your first stitch!

Slip Knot: For more info on how to make a slip knot, visit the Lion Brand® Yarn YouTube channel and search for the tutorial video titled "Getting Started: Slip Knot."

CASTING ON

Now, you're ready to cast on. There are many ways to cast on. Here's one super easy way:

Hold the needle with the slip knot in your left hand, with yarn tail to your left and ball yarn to your right. Slip the tip of right needle through the slip knot.

Wrap the ball yarn around your right index finger twice. This keeps the yarn under 'tension', so that your stitches won't be too loose or too tight.

Wrap the ball yarn around the right hand needle tip, counterclockwise.

Catch the wrapped yarn with the tip of the right hand needle and draw it through the loop, so you have a stitch on each of your needles.

Slide the new stitch from the right hand needle to the left hand needle. Pull gently on the yarn tail to tighten the stitch (don't make it too tight!)

Continue to cast on until you have the number of stitches in your pattern.

Casting On: For more info on how to cast on, visit the Lion Brand® Yarn YouTube channel and search for the tutorial video titled "How to Knit: Knitted Cast On."

KNIT STITCH

All "knitting" is made up of two basic stitches, the knit stitch and the purl stitch. The knit stitch is formed by putting your needle into the stitch from below.

Hold the needle with the cast on stitches in your left hand. Wrap the ball yarn over your right index finger.

Insert the tip of the right hand needle from front to back into the first stitch on the left hand needle. Wrap the ball yarn around right hand needle tip, counterclockwise.

Catch the wrapped yarn with the tip of the right hand needle and draw it through the loop. You have one stitch on your right hand needle!

Continue until you have knitted all the stitches from the left hand needle onto the right hand needle.

To begin the next row, switch the needles - so that the needle with the stitches on it is in your left hand.

WHAT'S GARTER STITCH? KNITTING EVERY STITCH ON EVERY ROW.

Knit Stitch: For more info on how to make a knit stitch, visit the Lion Brand® Yarn YouTube channel and search for the tutorial video titled "How to Knit: Knit Stitch."

PURL STITCH

The purl stitch is formed by putting your needle into the stitch from above, and from back to front.

Repeat Step 1 of the Knit stitch.

Repeat Step 2 of the Knit stitch, but insert the tip of the right hand needle from back to front.

Catch the wrapped yarn with the tip of the right hand needle and draw it through the loop. Now you have one stitch on your right hand needle.

Continue until you have knitted all the stitches from the left hand needle onto the right hand needle.

To begin the next row, switch the needles – so that the needle with the stitches on it is in your left hand.

WHAT'S STOCKINETTE STITCH? ALTERNATING ONE ROW OF KNIT STITCHES WITH ONE ROW OF PURL STITCHES.

Purl Stitch: For more info on how to make a purl stitch, visit the Lion Brand® Yarn YouTube channel and search for the tutorial video titled "How to Knit: Purl Stitch."

BINDING OFF Binding, or casting, off secures the stitches so they don't unravel when you are finished knitting.

When you're ready to end the piece you're working on, you need to bind off to secure all the stitches.

You can bind off in whatever stitch you were working in. If you were working just in the knit stitch, bind off in knit.

First, knit the first 2 stitches in the usual way. With the tip of your left hand needle, pick up the first stitch and lift it up and over the second stitch, then off the needle. This is one stitch bound off!

Knit the next stitch, then bind off just as on Step 3. Continue in this way until you have just one stitch remaining on your right hand needle.

Cut the yarn to about 8 inches and pull the yarn end through the last stitch to secure.

You have made your first piece of knitting!

Binding Off: For more info on how to bind off, visit the Lion Brand® Yarn YouTube channel and search for the tutorial video titled "How to Knit: Bind Off."

SEWING TWO GARTER STITCH PIECES TOGETHER The idea is to make your seams as "seamless" as possible. It takes practice to make completely invisible seams.

Thread a length of yarn into a blunt needle. Line up your 2 pieces, with the rows matching.

Beginning at one edge, draw the threaded needle through the bump made by the first row on one piece of knitting, then through the matching row on the other piece.

Continue sewing until the pieces are completely joined.

Weave in ends top and bottom.

'FINISHING' IS JUST WHAT IT SOUNDS LIKE- THE LAST STEP TO A COMPLETED PROJECT, AND THE THING THAT WILL MAKE YOUR PROJECT STURDY AND, WELL, FINISHED!

Seaming: For more info on how to sew garter stitch pieces together, visit the Lion Brand® Yarn YouTube channel and search for the tutorial video titled "How to Knit: WhipstitchGarter."

SEWING TWO STOCKINETTE STITCH PIECES TOGETHER

You can practice with a contrasting yarn, but on your actual project, use the yarn you knit with.

Thread a length of yarn into the tapestry needle. Line up the two pieces of fabric so the bottoms and tops are even.

Beginning at the bottom, whipstitch the pieces together so the sewing appears invisible.

Continue to the end.

ONCE YOU GET THE RHYTHM OF KNITTING AND PURLING, IT WILL BECOME SECOND NATURE. YOU'LL BE ABLE TO CHAT, WATCH TV, AND TAKE A MENTAL BREAK, AS NEEDED.

Seaming: For more info on how to sew stockinette stitch pieces together, visit the Lion Brand® Yarn YouTube channel and search for the tutorial video titled "How to Knit: WhipstitchStockinette."

WEAVING IN YARN ENDS When you get to the end of your project, sometimes you just want to be done! But weaving in the ends is the step that will make your piece look really finished, and keep it from unraveling, too.

Thread the yarn end into the blunt needle. Working on the wrong side of your piece, weave the threaded needle through the backs of several stitches, working in one direction, then the opposite direction.

Continue until you feel the yarn is secure.

When you're finished weaving the yarn end in, trim any excess length.

NOW THAT YOU KNOW THE FUNDAMENTALS OF KNITTING, IT'S TIME TO START ON A PROJECT. WE'VE SELECTED 7 GREAT BEGINNER PATTERNS WE THINK YOU'LL LOVE.

7 EASY PROJECTS

THREE-STRAND AFGHAN

BASIC BORDERED SCARF

SIMPLE SLOUCH HAT

STRIPED CHECKERBOARD BLANKET

TWO-STITCH COWL

LAPGHAN WITH POCKETS

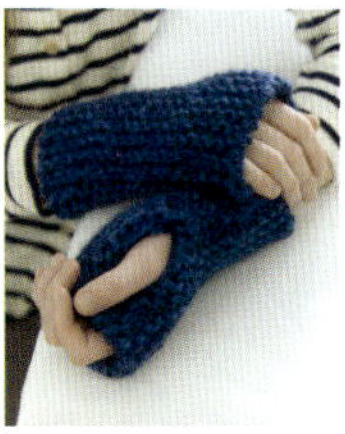

GARTER STITCH WRISTERS

MAKE IT!

THE YARN

#098 Houston Cream

THIS BASKET-WEAVE AFGHAN WILL KEEP ITS RECIPIENT COMFY FOR A LONG TIME!

THREE-STRAND AFGHAN

AFGHAN PATTERN MATERIALS

- LION BRAND® HOMETOWN USA® (Art. #135)
  #098 Houston Cream 18 balls or color of your choice
- LION BRAND® circular knitting needle size 35 (19 mm), 29 in. (73.5 cm) long
- LION BRAND® large-eyed blunt needle

SIZE

About 40 x 56 in. (101.5 x 142 cm)

GAUGE

5 stitches + 6 rows = about 4 in. (10 cm) over Rows 1-6 of pattern, working with 3 strands of yarn held together.
BE SURE TO CHECK YOUR GAUGE.

NOTES

1. Afghan is worked in one piece with 3 strands of yarn held together.
2. When you work with multiple strands, just hold all the strands together and knit as usual.
3. A circular needle is used to accommodate the large number of stitches. Work back and forth on the circular needle as if working on straight needles.

AFGHAN

With 3 strands of yarn held together, cast on 50 stitches.
Rows 1-6: *Knit 5, purl 5; repeat from * to end of row.
Rows 7-12: *Purl 5, knit 5; repeat from * to end of row.
Rows 13-84: Repeat Rows 1-12.
Bind off.

FINISHING

Weave in ends.

Every effort has been made to produce accurate and complete instructions. We cannot be responsible for variance of individual knitters or crocheters, human error, or typographical mistakes.

WORKING WITH CIRCULAR NEEDLES:

If you don't join the ends, you can use circular needles to knit flat pieces, just like you'd knit on straight needles.

You cast on to your circular needle in exactly the same way that you cast onto straight needles. After the stitches are cast on, hold the full needle (with all the cast-on sts on it) in your left hand and the empty needle in your right hand. Knit one row. Now you're going to change hands, as if you were knitting with two straight needles. Put the full needle in your left hand and the empty needle in your right hand, and knit (or purl) another row. At the end of every row just have the needles change hands so the empty needle is in your right hand.

MAKE IT!

THE YARN

#201 Ocean

A GREAT FIRST PROJECT, THIS CLASSIC SCARF IS BOTH EASY TO KNIT AND FUN TO WEAR.

BASIC BORDERED SCARF

SCARF PATTERN MATERIALS

- LION BRAND® HOMETOWN USA® (Art. #135)
  #201 Ocean 2 balls
  or color of your choice
- LION BRAND® knitting needles size 15 (10 mm)
- LION BRAND® stitch markers
- LION BRAND® large-eyed blunt needle

SIZE

About 8 x 60 in. (20.5 x 152.5 cm)

GAUGE

8 stitches = about 4 in. (10 cm)
in Stockinette stitch (knit on right side, purl on wrong side).
BE SURE TO CHECK YOUR GAUGE.

NOTES

1. Scarf is worked in one piece in Stockinette stitch with Garter stitch (knit every row) borders.
2. The edges of the finished Scarf may roll gently – this is not unusual with handknits!
3. Stitch markers are used to help you 'see' the stitches for the borders.

SCARF

Cast on 16 stitches.
Knit 6 rows. These 6 rows make the beginning Garter stitch border.
Next Row: Knit 2 for side edge border, place marker, knit to last 2 stitches for Stockinette stitch center section, place marker, knit 2 for side edge border.
Next Row: Knit 2, slip marker, purl to next marker, slip marker, knit 2.
Next Row: Knit 2, slip marker, knit to next marker, slip marker, knit 2.

Repeat the last 2 rows until the Scarf measures about 58 ½ in. (149 cm) from the beginning.
Next Row: Knit 2, remove marker, knit to next marker, remove marker, knit 2.
Knit 5 rows for the ending Garter stitch border.
Bind off.

FINISHING

Weave in ends.

Every effort has been made to produce accurate and complete instructions. We cannot be responsible for variance of individual knitters or crocheters, human error, or typographical mistakes.

MAKE IT!

THE YARN

#151 Katmai

CAN YOU BELIEVE THIS IS ACTUALLY A RECTANGLE SEWN UP AT THE SEAM AND GATHERED AT THE TOP?

SIMPLE SLOUCH HAT

HAT PATTERN MATERIALS

- LION BRAND® HEARTLAND® THICK & QUICK® (Art. #137)
  #151 Katmai 1 ball
  or color of your choice
- LION BRAND® knitting needles size 11 (8 mm)
- LION BRAND® large-eyed blunt needle

SIZE

Finished Circumference About 17 1/2 in. (44.5 cm), will stretch to fit a range of sizes.
Finished Length About 12 in. (30.5 cm)

GAUGE

11 stitches = about 4 in. (10 cm) in Stockinette stitch (knit on right side, purl on wrong side).
BE SURE TO CHECK YOUR GAUGE.

NOTES

1. Hat is worked in one piece in Stockinette stitch with a knit 1, purl 1 ribbed edge.
2. The top of the piece is gathered and the sides are sewn together to make the Hat.

HAT

Cast on 48 stitches.

Ribbed Edge

Row 1: *Knit 1, purl 1; repeat from * across the row.
Repeat Row 1 until the piece measures about 1 1/2 in. (4 cm) from the beginning.

Body of Hat

Next Row (right side): Knit across the row.
Next Row: Purl across the row.
Repeat the last 2 rows for Stockinette stitch until the piece measures about 12 in. (30.5 cm) from the beginning.

FINISHING

Cut yarn, leaving a yarn tail about 30 in. (76 cm) long. Thread the end of the yarn tail into the blunt needle.
Draw the threaded needle through the stitches on the knitting needle, one by one, sliding the stitches off the knitting needle as you draw the threaded needle through.
When all of the stitches are on the yarn tail, pull to gather the stitches together and close the top of the Hat.
Knot the yarn, then continuing with same yarn tail, sew the sides of the Hat together. Weave in ends.

Every effort has been made to produce accurate and complete instructions. We cannot be responsible for variance of individual knitters or crocheters, human error, or typographical mistakes.

MAKE IT!

THE YARN

#109 Olympic

#126 Sequoia

#135 Yosemite

#174 Joshua Tree

STRIPED CHECKERBOARD BLANKET

BLANKET PATTERN MATERIALS

- LION BRAND® HEARTLAND® THICK & QUICK® (Art. #137)
  - #174 Joshua Tree 2 balls (A)
  - #109 Olympic 2 balls (B)
  - #135 Yosemite 2 balls (C)
  - #126 Sequoia 2 balls (D)
  - or colors of your choice
- LION BRAND® circular needle size 11 (8 mm), 29 in. (73.5 cm) long
- LION BRAND® large-eyed blunt needle

SIZE

About 35 x 35 in. (89 x 89 cm)

GAUGE

11 stitches = about 4 in. (10 cm) over Rows 1-38 of pattern.
BE SURE TO CHECK YOUR GAUGE.

NOTES

1. Blanket is worked in one piece, changing yarn color every 36 rows to create stripes.
2. A circular needle is used to accommodate the large number of stitches. Work back and forth in rows on the circular needle, just as if working on straight needles.

BLANKET

With A, cast on 96 stitches.
Rows 1 and 2: Knit.
Row 3: Knit.
Row 4 (wrong side): Knit 25, purl 23, knit 23, purl 23, knit 2.
Rows 5-38: Repeat Rows 3 and 4.
Change to B.
Row 39 (right side): Knit.
Row 40: Knit 2, purl 23, knit 23, purl 23, knit 25.
Rows 41-74: Repeat Rows 39 and 40.
Change to C.
Repeat Rows 3-38.
Change to D.
Repeat Rows 39-74.
Knit 3 rows.
Bind off.

FINISHING

Weave in ends.

THIS HANDSOME BLANKET IS KNIT IN ONE PIECE ON A CIRCULAR NEEDLE.

THE YARN

#302 Aspen Tweed

A COZY COWL IS FLATTERING AND IS A GREAT GIFT FOR ANY AGE.

TWO-STITCH COWL

COWL PATTERN MATERIALS

- LION BRAND® HOMETOWN USA® (Art # 135)
  # 302 Aspen Tweed 2 balls
  or color of your choice
- LION BRAND® knitting needles size 13 (9 mm)
- LION BRAND® large-eyed blunt needle

SIZE

Finished Circumference About 28 in. (71 cm)
Finished Height About 10 in. (25.5 cm)

GAUGE

8 stitches = about 4 in. (10 cm) over pattern.
BE SURE TO CHECK YOUR GAUGE.

NOTES

1. Cowl is worked as a rectangle, then ends of piece are sewn together to make a ring.
2. The knit and purl stitches create an interesting texture on the cowl.

COWL

Cast on 55 stitches.
Row 1: *Knit 2, purl 2; repeat from * to last 3 stitches, knit 2, purl 1.
Repeat Row 1 for pattern until just 2 yd. (2 m) of yarn remains.
Bind off, but do not cut yarn.

FINISHING

Thread yarn end into blunt needle and sew sides of piece together for about 6 in. (15 cm), leaving remaining 4 in. (10 cm) unsewn for slit.

Weave in ends.

Every effort has been made to produce accurate and complete instructions. We cannot be responsible for variance of individual knitters or crocheters, human error, or typographical mistakes.

MAKE IT!

THE YARN

#173 Savannah Sage

#172 Oklahoma City Green

LAPGHAN WITH POCKETS

LAPGHAN PATTERN MATERIALS

- LION BRAND® HOMETOWN USA® (Art. #135)
  #173 Savannah Sage 5 balls (A)
  #172 Oklahoma City Green 1 ball (B)
  or colors of your choice
- LION BRAND® circular knitting needle size 13 (9 mm), 29 in. (73.5 cm) long
- LION BRAND® large-eyed blunt needle

SIZE

About 25 x 38 in. (63.5 x 96.5 cm)

GAUGE

9 stitches = about 4 in. (10 cm) in Stockinette stitch (knit on right side, purl on wrong side).
BE SURE TO CHECK YOUR GAUGE.

NOTES

1. The Lapghan is worked in one piece in Stockinette stitch with Garter stitch (knit every row) borders.
2. Two Pockets are worked separately in Garter stitch, then sewn to Lapghan.
3. A circular needle is used to accommodate the number of stitches on the Lapghan. Work back and forth on the circular needle just as if working on straight needles.

LAPGHAN

With A, cast on 56 stitches.
Knit 5 rows to make the beginning Garter stitch border.
Row 1: (wrong side): Knit 3 for the side border, purl across to the last 3 stitches for Stockinette stitch center section, knit the last 3 stitches for the side border.
Row 2: Knit.
Repeat Rows 1 and 2 until the piece measures about 37 in. (94 cm) from the beginning, ending with a Row 2 as the last row you work.
Knit 4 rows for the ending border.
Bind off.

POCKETS (Make 2)

With B, cast on 18 stitches.
Knit 40 rows.
Bind off.

FINISHING

Place a Pocket centered on the Lapghan, with the lower edge of the Pocket just inside the beginning Garter stitch border. Sew the lower and side edges of the Pocket to the Lapghan, leaving the top edge of the Pocket open. Sew the second Pocket to the opposite end of the Lapghan, with the lower edge of the Pocket just inside the ending Garter stitch border of the Lapghan.

Weave in ends.

MAKE IT!

THE YARN

#109 Olympic

YOU CAN TYPE, YOU CAN TEXT, AND YOU CAN EVEN KNIT WHEN YOU WEAR THESE EASY WRIST WARMERS.

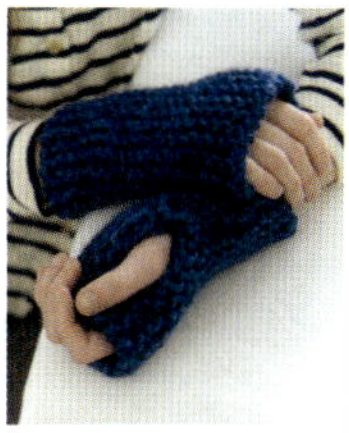

GARTER STITCH WRISTERS

WRISTERS PATTERN MATERIALS

- LION BRAND® HEARTLAND® THICK & QUICK® (Art. #137)
  #109 Olympic 1 ball
  or color of your choice
- LION BRAND® knitting needles size 11 (8 mm)
- LION BRAND® large-eyed blunt needle

SIZE

Finished Circumference About 7 in. (18 cm), will stretch to fit a range of sizes.
Finished Length About 7 in. (18 cm)

GAUGE

11 stitches = about 4 in. (10 cm) in Garter stitch (knit every row).
BE SURE TO CHECK YOUR GAUGE.

NOTES

1. Each Wrister is worked as a simple Garter stitch rectangle.
2. Each rectangle is sewn into a tube, leaving an opening for thumb.

WRISTERS (Make 2)

Cast on 19 stitches.
Work in Garter stitch until the piece measures about 7 in. (18 cm) from the beginning.
Bind off.

FINISHING

Cut yarn, leaving a yarn tail about 18 in. (45.5 cm) long. Thread the end of the yarn tail into the blunt needle.
Fold the piece, bringing the cast on edge to meet the bound off edge.
With the threaded blunt needle, sew the edges together, leaving a 2 in. (5 cm) opening for thumb.

Weave in ends.

WHAT ELSE CAN I MAKE?

ALL OF THE PROJECTS IN THIS BOOKLET ARE SUPER SIMPLE TO MAKE so that your introduction to knitting is as stress-free as possible. After all, as a caregiver you are already under enough pressure, and we want knitting to minimize your stress level, not add to it!

As we've mentioned, adding increasing and decreasing will give you lots more project options once you are ready to tackle more advanced projects and techniques. But for now, here are some other easy, fun and useful items you can make from squares and rectangles, with the two basic stitches you have learned in this booklet.

- **COASTERS** Basically a 4 in. x 4 in. swatch, knit up several squares and tie a ribbon around them as a quick gift for someone who has done a good deed for you.

- **LAP ROBES, SHAWLS, SCARVES AND THROWS** In addition to the ones we've included in this booklet, there are tons of patterns for easy designs on lionbrand.com.

- **TOTE BAGS** Knit up a rectangle, fold it in half, sew the seams, add a ribbon handle, and, bingo, you have a handmade tote bag to keep future knitting projects in!

- **PILLOWS** Add some duplicate stitch, an applique heart or some playful buttons to a plain stockinette square or rectangle, back it with some fabric and you have a custom pillow. (It's easy to find pillow inserts at craft or fabric shops.) What a nice way to cheer up a hospital room. To learn duplicate stitch, visit: www.lionbrand.com/faq/253

FOR THESE AND MORE THAN 6000 FREE PATTERNS, VISIT LIONBRAND.COM

• **WASHCLOTHS AND DISHCLOTHS** These practical and fun-to-knit items make much-appreciated gifts and are perfect on-the-go projects. Put together a spa basket with some nice soaps, creams and aromatherapy oils for someone you know who needs a little pampering.

• **LEGWARMERS** Measure the length of the leg from just below the knee to just above the ankle, and the circumference of the calf. Subtract two inches to allow for stretch. (in other words, if the calf measures 12" make the rectangle 10" wide.) Knit two rectangles, and seam each one along the long side. Try adding some crochet trim around the top and bottom edges.

• **ANYTHING PATCHWORK** For a distraction during frequent hospital visits and doctor appointments, just set a goal of "Today I will make one (or two) 4" squares". Before you know it, you'll have enough squares to make a gorgeous patchwork blanket.

• **TECH PROTECTION** Covers for your cell phone, iPad or computer are super easy to whip up and customize.

TIP: Squares are a great place to experiment with different stitch patterns and combinations Once you've mastered the basics, use different combos of knit and purl stitches to create different textures.

RESOURCES

Get the Scoop!

WEBSITES, BLOGS, AND OTHER ON-LINE KNITTING RESOURCES:

CRAFT YARN COUNCIL Since the mid 1990s the Craft Yarn Council (CYC) has surveyed hundreds of thousands of knitters and crocheters about why they enjoy these crafts. Stress relief ranks at the top, along with creative fulfillment. CYC's website contains resources, including a video about the therapeutic benefits of knitting and crocheting. In addition, a growing number of studies have been completed and articles written about the benefits of knitting and crochet to one's mood, mind and body. **www.craftyarncouncil.com**

KNIT FREEDOM Personal blog of a woman who recovered from an eating disorder through knitting. **http://knit-freedom.com/personal-journey/knit-ting-and-health-back-in-new**

LION BRAND WELLNESS BLOG
The well-known yarn company's website provides patterns, yarn-themed e-cards, forums where yarncrafters can share and discuss topics, and many more helpful resources. Of particular note is their Wellness blog where testimonials and stories highlight the therapeutic benefits of knitting and crochet. **blog.lionbrand.com/category/wellness/**

LOVEKNITTING This blog has a terrific post from "Time to Talk (about mental illness) Day" about the therapeutic benefits of knitting; **blog.loveknitting.com/time-to-talk-day-the-health-benefits-of-knitting**

RAVELRY Free online pattern library, marketplace, and community for knitters and crocheters. Yarncrafters can connect with one another and find everything from help with pattern directions to information on local knitting groups and yarn stores, and more. **www.ravelry.com**

STITCHLINKS "The home of therapeutic knitting since 2005," the site promotes the use of therapeutic knitting and stitching through research, and promotes crafting and certain other activities as a means of keeping people mentally active, motivated and socially engaged. **www.stitchlinks.com**